75

a special gift for

_____

IN APPRECIATION
FOR ALL YOU DO

_____

DATE

_____

Stories, sayings, and scriptures to Encourage and Inspire

hugs™

for
Nurses

PHILIS
BOULTINGHOUSE

Personalized Scriptures by
LEANN WEISS

HOWARD BOOKS
A DIVISION OF SIMON & SCHUSTER

New York London Toronto Sidney

DEDICATION

to my wonderful mother-in-law,
NELDA BOULTINGHOUSE,
who served as a nurse
for thirty years,
giving of herself and
endearing herself
to countless patients
and their families

Our purpose at Howard Books is to:

- *Increase faith* in the hearts of growing Christians
- *Inspire holiness* in the lives of believers
- *Instill hope* in the hearts of struggling people everywhere

Because He's coming again!

HOWARD
BOOKS

Published by Howard Books, a division of Simon & Schuster
1230 Avenue of the Americas, New York, NY 10020

Hugs for Nurses © 2003 by Philis Boultinghouse

Library of Congress Cataloging-in-Publication Data
Boultinghouse, Philis, 1951–
  Hugs for nurses : stories, sayings, and scriptures to encourage and inspire / Philis Boultinghouse ; personalized scriptures by LeAnn Weiss.
    p. cm.
 ISBN: 1-58229-280-9
      1. Nurses—Religious life. 2. Nursing—Religious aspects—Christianity. I. Weiss, LeAnn. II. Title.

BV4596.N8 B68 2003
242'.68—dc21

2002038752

20 19 18 17 16 15 14 13 12 11

HOWARD is a registered trademark of Simon & Schuster, Inc.

Manufactured in the United States of America

For information regarding special discounts for bulk purchases, please contact Simon & Schuster Special Sales at 1-800-456-6798 or business@simonandschuster.com.

Thanks to Debra Eldridge, Laura Fletcher, and Wanda Fuller for sharing their stories with me. Thanks to Nelda Boultinghouse and Laura Fletcher who served as professional consultants.

Paraphrased scriptures © 2003 LeAnn Weiss, 3006 Brandywine Dr., Orlando, FL 32806; 407-898-4410

Edited by Between the Lines
Interior design by Stephanie Denney
Illustrations by Misty McKeithen

contents

love

CHAPTER
one

1

May you realize My love for you, which
infinitely supersedes anything you've
ever experienced or dreamed. I rise up
and help you, redeeming you because
of My unfailing and ever-present love.
When you love others, I live in you
and My love is made complete in you.
May your life be completely filled with
My blessings.

My endless love,

YOUR HEAVENLY
FaTHer

—from Ephesians 3:17–19; Psalm 44:26; 1 John 4:12

The Bible says it very simply: *"Faith, hope, and love—but the greatest of these is love."* In a very basic sense, nursing is a profession of loving: Love means giving of yourself to others, and that's what you do every single day.

You don't always know what challenges will greet you at the beginning of your workday, but you do know that you will be called upon to give of yourself; you know that every day, in ways big or small, you will be called upon to love.

Some of the patients you meet are a joy to serve. In fact, some who sit or lie at the other end of your stethoscope actually bring joy to you. Then inspirational message

there are those who challenge your patience
at every turn, who have no appreciation for the
service you render. Often those patients are the ones
who need your love the most—and you are up to the
challenge, for your chosen profession is one of giving—
one of love.

Your love is shared through the assurance of your
smile, the tenderness of your touch, the kindness of
your voice. Taking time to explain a difficult
procedure, holding the hand of a frightened
child, sitting with a family as they wait…
all of these are expressions of love.
This is who you are and what you
do every day.

5

Love cures
people, the
ones who
receive love
and the ones
who give it,
too.

KARL A. MENNINGER

As Annie's mother's heart pulled further and further away, Marcie's heart moved closer in.

special only

Little Annie wasn't much different from the hundreds of other tiny babies who'd come through the neonatal intensive care unit of Morris Memorial Hospital. Just like all the others, she was dangerously below normal birthweight. She weighed just three pounds, eight ounces when she was born. Like the other premature babies, her heart and lungs were underdeveloped. And like other preemies, little Annie had numerous tubes invading her tiny body, carrying precious nutrients and medications into her fragile system. She also had probes and wires attached to her paper-thin skin, monitoring her heart rate, temperature, pulse, and oxygen levels.

Love

But for all her similarities to her NICU cohabitants, there was something different about Annie.

Annie was alone.

The visiting hours in NICU were very strict—nine to ten o'clock in the morning, four to five in the afternoon, nine to ten in the evening, and one to two in the morning. All the other babies in the unit were visited regularly. Weary moms and dads and concerned grandmas and grandpas made daily visits to the isolated unit to stroke, sing to, or simply feast their eyes upon their beloved offspring. They cooed softly, touched gently, and cried silently.

Some of the babies were so sick and so small that physical touch was too much stimulation for their underdeveloped nervous systems. But even the parents of these babies came to gaze longingly on the objects of their affection, willing the tiny bodies to grow and become strong.

In the beginning Annie's mother had come with the rest. But she always came alone. No friends or family ever accompanied her. No husband, no grandparents—no one. During her visits, she spent more time looking around the room or at the other babies than she did looking at Annie.

She would stand by Annie's Isolette, leaning on it a little, looking forlorn and hopeless. She didn't ask questions like the other parents did; she didn't touch or talk to her tiny little girl. She came to the hospital out of a manufactured sense of duty, and she had no intentions of getting attached to the baby that, deep down, she knew she wouldn't take home.

It wasn't just that she didn't expect Annie to live; she had no desire to take on the responsibility of caring for this needy human being. Her visits became more and more sporadic until, eventually, she didn't come at all.

But Annie wasn't completely alone.

There was someone who cared, someone who stood by her Isolette and gazed longingly at her, someone who stroked her spindly legs and hummed sweet songs in the night. Marcie was an NICU nurse who worked the night shift. She watched Annie's mother during the first few weeks; she saw her growing detachment and her gradual decision not to love her baby. And as Annie's mother's heart pulled further and further away, Marcie's heart moved closer in.

Love

In some ways Marcie identified with Annie. Like Annie, Marcie had no one in her life who cared just for her. Sure, she had friends and family—lots of people who loved her in a general sort of way—but since her husband's death two years ago, Marcie had come to the awful realization that she was no one's "special only."

Annie's need to be someone's "special only" touched Marcie deeply. Marcie had no idea how she would make it happen, but her resolve to see that this baby was loved and cared for grew with each passing day.

Yet it was the night Annie was crying inconsolably and couldn't be comforted by the usual methods that Marcie's resolve became personal. Annie now weighed five pounds and was strong enough to be held. NICU babies who had no regular visitors were routinely rocked by volunteer aides during the day, but at night it was the nurses who rocked the babies as they had time, and Marcie always volunteered to rock Annie.

It wasn't difficult to persuade the other nurses to pass on Annie. Annie's mother had been a heavy drinker, and her alcohol consumption had left Annie with fetal alcohol syndrome. You could already see some physical signs of the disease: a small head, drooping eyelids, and a thin upper lip. Though the abnormalities were not severe, Annie didn't have the same "cute" appeal as the other babies in the unit.

On this particular night, Annie's shrill, incessant screaming was agitating not only the other babies but the entire nursing staff as well. Marcie had finished most of her routine duties, so she offered to take Annie from the frustrated nurse who was walking and bouncing the screeching bundle in a futile attempt to quiet her. The weary nurse willingly gave her up.

Marcie dragged a rocking chair into the supply room, pulled the door shut—leaving it open just a bit so she could see—and turned off the bright overhead light. Cradling little Annie in her arms, she rocked her gently back and forth…back and forth. Marcie improvised a lullaby as she rocked: "It's time to go to sleep; it's time to close your eyes. It's time to lay your head down and go to sleep, my darling." But Annie's cries only intensified, and her tiny body arched and

Love

stiffened. No matter how Marcie rocked or held or positioned her, Annie continued to cry. Marcie was running out of ideas.

Then she remembered a technique she'd learned in nursing school years ago—it was something she'd taught many mothers to do but had never had the opportunity to do herself. It was called "kangaroo care." Marcie unwrapped Annie's blanket and draped it over the arm of the rocking chair; then she removed Annie's hospital-issue pink gown, leaving her clad in only her diaper and warming hat. Almost timidly, Marcie unbuttoned the bottom half of her scrub shirt and placed little Annie against her bare abdomen. Then she loosely closed her shirt around the baby to keep her warm and resumed her rocking and quiet singing.

Annie's fierce screams subsided almost immediately, and her little body seemed to melt into Marcie's. A peaceful warmth filled Marcie. She was profoundly aware of the need of this helpless human being for someone to love her constantly and unconditionally—someone who would love her as a "special only." And Marcie was just as aware of her own need for someone to love.

Skin to skin, the two of them rocked together in quiet

bliss for nearly half an hour. Thinking Annie was asleep, Marcie opened her shirt and laid Annie on her lap as she reached for the little pink gown. But Annie's eyes were wide open, and she stared lovingly up into Marcie's. Not wanting to shatter the moment, Marcie covered Annie in her little blanket and returned her intense gaze. At that moment, two lonely souls connected—it was a spark that ignited Marcie's imagination and fired her determination to take this baby into her life—to care for her and raise her as her own, to love her as her "special only."

Marcie had no idea what the adoption process would entail, but she felt a peace and resolve that the desire of her heart would become a reality. Marcie was no longer gazing into the eyes of one baby among many; she was gazing into the eyes of her "special only"—the eyes of the tiny baby she knew with all her heart would one day be her daughter.

Marcie's dream became a reality six months later when she stood before the judge who signed the final adoption papers. Cradling her precious daughter in her arm, streams of tears flowing down her face, Marcie signed the papers that declared Annie and Marcie each other's "special only."

peace

CHAPTER
TWO

17

You have access to peace with Me through Jesus. Each day I carry your burdens. When you trust in and focus on Me, I'll bless you with My perfect peace that will relieve your fears, even in the most difficult trials and circumstances. Always be prepared to gently and respectfully give an answer to everyone who asks about the source of your hope.

Lifting you up,

Y O U R   G O D   O F

peace

—from Romans 5:1; Psalm 68:19; Isaiah 26:3; Philippians 4:6–7; 1 Peter 3:15–16

Illness and pain have a way of stripping away all that's trivial and unimportant and bringing to the surface all that really matters. Some patients under your care may be going through deep periods of soul searching. They may need answers to questions they've never asked before. Some of those you care for will look to you for words of encouragement and peace. Sometimes they'll simply need the assurance that tomorrow will be brighter and that healing is on its way. At other times they'll long to know deeper truths and a peace that endures.

The peace we all long for is a state of mind and a matter of the heart. It's a serenity and a calmness that can be sensed and seen, shared and spoken. But as caregivers and ambassadors of peace, we may sometimes feel that peace has eluded our own hearts. We can't share with others what we don't have ourselves. At these times we must go to the source of all peace and renew ourselves so we can bring peace to others out of our own overflow. In the Book of Psalms, King David promised, *"The* LORD *gives strength to his people; the* LORD *blesses his people with peace"* (Psalm 29:11).

Because of who you are and what you do, you share a tranquillity of spirit and a peaceful assurance that tomorrow is coming—and with it, healing, health, and peace.

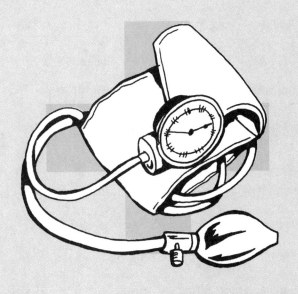

Within the
reach of every
Christian is
the unending
presence
of God.

MAX LUCADO

Although Laura was
pretty, it wasn't her
looks that attracted
Jake to her; he saw in
her the kind of peace
he desperately desired.

Rescued at Heart

Jake was gorgeous. He had thick, curly, black hair, lively green eyes, and a tightly toned, muscular body. He was the kind of guy girls turned to watch as he sauntered by. He prided himself on his ability to "attract the ladies," as he'd coyly say.

But his life was changed forever one afternoon during a leisurely swim. It wasn't his charm that he lost—or his good looks. It was his ability to saunter. In fact, after that infamous day, he couldn't move—or feel—anything below his shoulders.

peace

Jake was a military policeman at Fort Polk, Louisiana. On a Sunday afternoon, he and some military buddies had gone swimming in a nearby lake with some civilian girls. There were six of them altogether—three guys and three girls. They swam and skied until evening.

As they headed back to town in the open Jeep, with the wind blowing through their hair, Jake reveled in the intoxication of the carefree afternoon. When one of the girls said she hadn't quite gotten her fill of swimming, Jake knew just what to do. Instead of turning back toward the lake, he headed for the base and the restricted-access pool that glistened invitingly from behind the forbidding fence. Feeling full of himself and sure of his "privileges" as an MP, Jake was not deterred by the "KEEP OUT" sign posted on the locked gate. He whipped the Jeep alongside the fence, jumped up on its hood, and extended his hand gallantly to his girl.

Soon all six of them were swimming and splashing in the warm, clean water. It was a perfect ending to a perfect day...

No one remembered hearing a splash. No one saw him

hit. Just minutes before, Jake had been showing off his diving prowess. Then the other two guys, trying to get some attention for themselves, started an underwater wrestling match. The girls were giggling and squealing as the young men splashed and roughhoused in the shallow end of the pool. Jake must have lost his balance and hit his head on the diving board. When one of the others finally turned around, Jake was floating facedown in the water.

+ + + + +

Jake awoke lying flat on his back, staring into a pair of beautiful, deep blue eyes. "And who are you, pretty lady?" Jake flirted with all the charisma he could muster.

"My name is Laura, Mr. Alexander," she stated professionally but with a twinkle in her eye. "Nurse Laura."

Jake watched Nurse Laura lift his wrist to check his pulse, but he couldn't feel a thing. *Strange,* he thought. *How could I not feel the touch of a beautiful woman like this?*

Wait a minute! He thought with sudden panic, *Why am I in a room with a nurse? And why is she checking my pulse?*

Jake looked quickly around the room, assessing his

surroundings. The beige walls were devoid of pictures or homeyness of any kind. Instead a small, black television was mounted high on the wall, and an ugly metal supply cabinet stood in the corner. It was then that he noticed the numerous carts and the overwhelming array of beeping machines. They were everywhere—maybe ten or more. Tubes and wires of all sorts emanated from each machine, and they all ran toward a central location. With horror he realized that he was that center. All the tubes and wires were running into his body!

Laura bent down so she could look Jake straight in the eye. She'd learned from years of working with debilitated patients how much they appreciated her getting down on their level instead of hovering over them, making them feel detached and almost inhuman.

"Jake, do you know what happened to you?" Laura asked gently, her eyes searching his.

Jake's head began to swim as he tried to piece his memories together. He saw flashes of light glistening off clear water; he remembered sounds of delicious laughter and playful splashing. He remembered bouncing on the diving board, extending his arms above his head, shaping his body into perfect form. Then a twist of his ankle—balance lost, his body contorting…

That was it. That was all he could remember.

He returned Laura's gaze, his eyes registering growing understanding then rising horror as he started to grasp the truth about his unresponsive body and pounding head.

"NO!" he yelled. "I don't know what happened to me! Why can't I move my legs?" He shook his head violently. Increasing terror filled his eyes. "And why can't I move my arms—I can't even feel them! What's going on? Why am I here?" His voice rose to a frightened wail.

Jake's loud ranting brought the attending physician bursting through the door.

"Calm down, Mr. Alexander," the doctor said firmly. "There's no need for such a commotion. You should be thankful that you're alive."

Jake's head flailed from side to side in agitation. His mind screamed commands to every muscle in his body to jump

CHAPTER TWO
peace

out of bed and run out the door, but only his head and shoulders responded.

Laura stepped aside gracefully when the doctor breezed past her; but she kept her eyes riveted on Jake, ready to communicate compassion and calm should he look her way.

"What happened to me?" Jake howled.

"If you'll calm down and quit carrying on, I'll tell you what happened," the dispassionate doctor said.

Jake looked intently at the doctor without saying a word, his eyes narrowed and set.

"Apparently, you hit your head when you dove into a pool. You fractured the C4 and C5 vertebrae of your spine, instantly rendering yourself a quadriplegic. You're permanently paralyzed from your shoulders down. You also aspirated some water, causing an infection in your lungs. On the bright side, if you had broken the next vertebra up—your C3—you wouldn't have been able to breathe on your own—ever. As I said, you're very lucky to be alive," the doctor concluded dryly.

"Nurse," the doctor said, noticing Laura for the first time, "explain to this patient the course of his treatment and what he can expect." With this, he turned his back on his frightened patient and left.

Laura gently touched Jake's forehead—one of the few places he could still feel. Her kind touch was a stark contrast to the doctor's harsh demeanor. At her touch, tears streamed from Jake's eyes—tears of fear, frustration, and gratitude. Laura reexplained—much more gently—what the doctor had said.

Over the next several weeks, Jake slowly adjusted to his new state of life. He began to relax a little, and his charm resurfaced. Laura, of course, was his favorite nurse.

Whenever he faced a difficult procedure, he would whine like a baby, then wink and grin at Laura. "Such a charmer," she would say with a smile.

One day Jake struck a deal with Laura. "Want to know how to get me to be a more cooperative patient?"

Laura was afraid to ask, but she couldn't resist his smile. "And how would I do that, Mr. Alexander?" she asked, her eyes filled with laughter.

"M&M's," he said simply. "I love M&M's."

"Now how did I get by all this time without knowing that you love M&M's?" Laura asked.

"Well, I was saving that important piece of information for just the right time. My very favorite is the kind in the orange package with the peanut butter in the middle. Not the kind with the peanuts inside and not the plain kind— the kind with peanut butter in the center. You got it?"

"Yes, smarty-pants, I got it."

For all of Jake's joviality, he still had serious physical problems. Unable to clear the fluid from his lungs, he suffered from numerous life-threatening lung infections. But Jake fought hard to live.

Part of his will to live came from his indomitable spirit, but there was something more. Contrary to appearances, Jake wasn't at peace—not with himself and not with God. And deep in his heart he wanted to be at peace with his maker before he left this life.

It was his desire for peace that attracted him to Laura. He'd known many women in his life, and most of those relationships had been based on physical attraction. Although

Laura was pretty, it wasn't her looks that attracted Jake to her; he saw in her the kind of peace he desperately desired.

And it was his craving for peace that moved Jake to lay aside his facade of charm and wit and ask Laura about the source of the peace and light he saw in her.

"I'm glad you asked," she answered gently. "I bought you a gift a few days ago, and I've been waiting for just the right time to share it with you." Within minutes she returned with a small box from which she lifted a black, leather Bible. As she held it up to Jake's face, he saw that his name had been engraved on the bottom right corner. His eyes filled with warm tears of acceptance as he smiled his appreciation.

That night Laura shared with him her faith and read comforting passages from the Book of Psalms. She told Jake about God and about how she'd come to trust Him as her Father; and for the first time in Jake's life, he began to believe that there might be a God—and more amazingly, that He might love him.

Jake finally fell into a peaceful sleep—the most peaceful sleep he'd had since he was a child. When he awoke the

peace

next morning, he instinctively turned toward the door to look for Laura. But something on the bedstand caught his eye. It was the new Bible Laura had given him, and on top of the Bible was a mound of orange packages of peanut butter M&M's.

A seed of peace had been planted in his heart, and Jake knew he would never be the same.

comfort

CHAPTER
THREE

35

I am He who comforts you! By My amazing grace, I've given you eternal encouragement and good hope. I encourage your heart and strengthen you in every good word and deed. I make your life rich in every way that counts so that you can be generous at all times. Make a habit of encouraging and building everyone up daily. Your generous spirit will result in thanksgiving to Me.

Comforting hugs,

YOUR FAITHFUL

GOD

—from Isaiah 51:12; 2 Thessalonians 2:16–17;
2 Corinthians 9:11; 1 Thessalonians 5:11

One of the greatest gifts you give ailing patients is comfort. How often have you heard or said, "Just try to make her (or him) comfortable."

But you know better than the average person that comfort goes beyond the physical realm. Broken hearts are just as serious—if not more so—as broken bones. Fear of the unknown, concern about the future, anxiety about family and work, and how illness will affect others—these issues trouble the hearts of those under your care, those needing your touch of comfort.

Some of those for whom you care harbor pain in their hearts that may manifest itself in rude behavior,

outbursts of anger, or irrational conduct. They
might cause you to momentarily forget the joy of
serving others. You might feel undervalued and unap-
preciated. In times like these, *you* may need to be comforted. And God, your heavenly Father, will do just
that: *"The Father of compassion and the God of all comfort…comforts us in all our troubles, so that we can comfort those in any trouble with the comfort we ourselves
have received from God"* (2 Corinthians 1:3–4).

You, the giver of comfort, are comforted by
a loving heavenly Father so that out of the
overflow of that comfort, you may comfort others—no matter how they
behave.

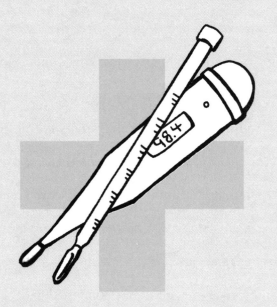

Love is
most divine
when it
loves
according
to needs,
and not
according to
merit.

GEORGE MACDONALD

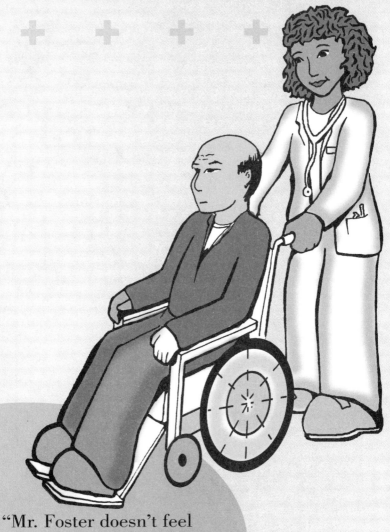

"Mr. Foster doesn't feel good all right, but his bad feeling is mostly in his heart, not his head."

Happy Heart

Elizabeth slammed her clipboard as hard as she dared onto the nurses' station desk as she let out an exasperated, "Ahhhh!"

"That Mr. Foster in 328 is about to drive me over the edge! No matter what I do, it's wrong. If I try to arrange his pillows to make him more comfortable, he tells me to leave him alone—they were just right the way they were, and now he won't be able to get them right again if he works at it all day. If I come into the room without attempting to fluff them, he bellows at me for sloughing off on the job and not caring that he has to lie on a hard bed on hard, flat pillows. I've had it!"

Karen looked up from her computer screen. "I know what you mean. The other day, when the dietary technician delivered his food, he lifted the cover, and when he saw what it was, he actually picked up the plate and threw it across the room, screaming, 'Can't you incompetent imbeciles get anything right?!' The poor woman ran out of the room crying. Now none of the cafeteria workers will take his food in. They're terrified of him. They just leave it outside his door, and one of us takes it in. We inform him what's under the cover and ask if he wants it. If he gripes about it, we just take it away and don't worry about it. If he wants to go hungry, that's his choice."

Elizabeth was a registered nurse in the medical surgery unit at Norman County Regional. Most days she loved her job. She'd been on this same floor, in this same hospital for nine years. Some of her coworkers viewed their time in the surgery unit as a steppingstone to something more exciting or "significant," but Elizabeth liked the idea of helping people recover from surgery. Though usually lasting only a few days, recovery was a big ordeal for each patient, and Elizabeth enjoyed playing the role of comforter—if only for a short time and in small ways.

Just next door to Mr. Foster was a little girl who was the antithesis of the cranky Mr. Foster. And for all her cheerfulness, she had reason to be grumpy. Nine-year-old Amber was recovering from her sixth surgery. She had a congenital heart condition that had required multiple surgeries as her body grew. But somehow, through it all, she had maintained a sunny outlook on life.

Elizabeth took special pleasure in tending to Amber. Amber enjoyed arts and crafts, so every time she came in for a hospital stay, Elizabeth planned some fun project for her to do. This time, since Valentine's Day was coming soon, she had taught her how to make pop-up heart cards by folding a strip of paper accordion style and gluing one end to the construction-paper card and the other end to a cut-out heart. When the card was closed, the heart would lie flat inside, but when it was opened, the heart would spring up.

"Hi, sweetheart!" Elizabeth chirped as she entered Amber's room.

Amber had construction paper, crayons, and scissors spread out on her food tray.

"I see you're making some Valentines," Elizabeth said encouragingly.

"Kind of," Amber replied. "I decided to make some happy-heart get-well cards for the other patients. They're not just Valentine's Day cards; they're cards to help their hearts feel happy so they can get well faster. I saw on TV that when you're happy, it helps your body get strong faster. Did you know that?"

"Yes," said Elizabeth, "I've heard something like that myself." *What a sweet child*, Elizabeth thought. *That Mr. Foster should be ashamed of himself! He's had one minor surgery, and he'll be out of the hospital in a day or two. This child has had six and will likely have to endure another one within the year!*

"I'm making a special one for that man next door," Amber continued. "I think I heard him crying last night. I'm making a happy-heart card to cheer him up!"

Elizabeth couldn't restrain herself; she leaned over and gave Amber a big, proud hug. "Amber, you are one amazing little girl! If anyone can brighten Mr. Foster's heart, you're the one! I'll be glad to give him the card when you're finished."

"Oh, I don't want *you* to give the card to him; I want to give it to him *myself*."

"Oh," Elizabeth said hesitantly, not sure how to explain Mr. Foster's ill temper to this nine-year-old optimist. "I don't know if that's such a good idea. He has headaches a lot of the time."

"I know about the plate of food."

"What are you talking about?" Elizabeth asked, feigning confusion.

"Don't try to trick me, Nurse Lizzy. I'm not a little kid! I heard him screaming, and I heard the plate crash against my wall, and I heard that food lady crying and running out of the room. Mr. Foster doesn't feel good all right, but his bad feeling is mostly in his heart, not his head."

Out of the mouths of babes..., Elizabeth thought.

Later that day as she passed Mr. Foster's room, Elizabeth heard an unfamiliar voice. "Dad, we've got to get this settled. Mom would want us to."

"Don't try to tell me what your mother would want us to do!" Mr. Foster shouted. "I lived with your mother for fifty-one years; I know what your mother would want!"

"I just…"

"Just give me a little more time," he said a little more quietly now…and a great deal more sadly. "She's only been gone a month. It can wait a few more weeks. She's only been gone a month…"

So that's it. How could I have judged him so harshly without considering what might be going on in his life? No wonder he's angry all the time. Only little Amber saw past the exterior behavior and into his heart. I can't even imagine the pain… Elizabeth's thoughts drifted as she thought about her own spouse of ten years. She couldn't begin to fathom how she would feel—and act—if she lost her Jim.

About twenty minutes later she heard another voice coming from room 328. It was the voice of little Amber. Elizabeth sidled up to the open door and peeked around the corner.

"I made this card for you," Amber said to the back of Mr. Foster's head.

Mr. Foster continued to stare out the window.

"Excuse me, sir," Amber tried again, a little louder this time, "I made a card for you."

Mr. Foster turned his head slowly toward the little intruder. "What are you doing in my room? Who gave you permission to come in here?" he demanded irritably.

But brave Amber was undaunted. "First of all, I already told you why I'm in your room. I came here to give you a card. And to answer your second question, no one gave me permission; I just came. My room is next to yours, so it's kind of like we're neighbors. My name is Amber Brownlow, and I have a congenital heart condition. Do you know what *congenital* means?"

"Yes, I know what *congenital* means," he said with a fading gruffness.

"Well," Amber continued without missing a beat, "I've had six surgeries on my heart, so I know what it's like to be a patient, and I've started a project—I'm calling it Happy Heart Cards. I'm making cards for some of the other patients to cheer them up, and you're the very first one to get a Happy Heart card." With this, she ceremoniously extended the red construction-paper card.

Mr. Foster could hardly refuse. As he opened the card, the red paper heart sprang out to greet him. He couldn't help but smile. He read aloud,

> A happy heart is a healthy heart,
> And this is what I pray for you:
> That your heart POPS back to strength
> And you'll be happy through and through.

Mr. Foster's heart melted in an instant, and unexpected tears sprang to his eyes.

"Thank you, Amber," he said softly. "This is the best present I've gotten in a very long time. Will you come back and see me again tomorrow and bring your own happy heart with you? I think it's just the medicine I need."

"Sure, Mr. Foster. And maybe you can help me make some Happy Heart cards for some of the other patients."

"I'd be glad to," he said warmly.

Elizabeth slipped quietly away from the door, thankful to have witnessed this tender exchange—and inspired by the reminder that even the gloomiest patients need her unconditional gift of comfort—no matter how they behave.

hope

CHAPTER
Four

51

You can count on Me! My legacy continues through all generations. I'm loving toward you and 100 percent faithful to all of My promises. I'm transforming you into My likeness with an ever-increasing glory. Let your soul wait upon Me, and put your hope in My eternal Word, which firmly stands in the heavens. Surely My absolute goodness and love will follow you each and every day of your life.

My everlasting promise,

YOUR HEAVENLY

FATHER

—from Psalm 145:13; 2 Corinthians 3:18;
Psalms 130:5; 119:89; 23:6

You are an ambassador of hope. Each time you walk into a patient's room, you bring the possibility of comfort, relief, or long-awaited information. When a body is sick, it's easy for a mind to become anxious or filled with despair. Every day you show up for work, you help ease worried minds and restore fragile hope.

When you take a few moments to answer questions left unanswered by busy doctors, you revive hope. When you assure a patient that tomorrow will be better than today, you engender hope. When your confident voice reminds a patient that it's perfectly normal to feel this way, you build hope. You are a person of great value.

And sometimes the ones you care for need

a deeper hope—an eternal hope. Here, too, you

can be an ambassador. As you rely on God, He will

supply you with hope enough for yourself and for those

you serve. This is the apostle Paul's prayer for you:

"May the God of hope fill you with all joy and peace as

you trust in him, so that you may overflow with hope by

the power of the Holy Spirit" (Romans 15:13).

As a caregiver, you have an enormous task.

But you are not left to accomplish it alone.

As your job calls you to supply hope to

others, the God of the universe will

fill you with all the hope you'll

need.

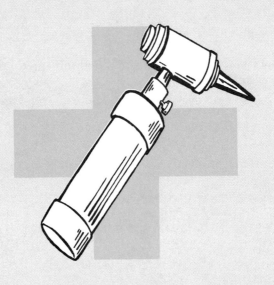

Hope helps us lift our eyes off the broken pieces in front of us to see the big picture God is working in our lives.

KIRK SULLIVAN

Lette bowed her head,
and every head in the
room bowed reverently
with her.

LETTE'S LEGACY

Lette sat on the edge of Lodell's bed, gazing tenderly into the eyes of the woman who had become her friend.

Lette was the home-healthcare nurse assigned to Lodell Wright's case. Just five-foot-two, Lette wore her gray hair in a tight bun at the nape of her neck. A casual onlooker might assess her daily attire—usually a long, dark-colored skirt and an outdated floral blouse—and assume she was a rather *drab* persona. But anyone who spent more than five minutes with her quickly saw that the radiance of her spirit and the brightness of her smile seemed to make her *glow*.

CHAPTER FOUR

HOPE

Lette's job was to make Lodell as comfortable as possible. But Lette did much more. She tended to the needs of her patient's spirit. She answered the questions that haunted Lodell, spoke soothing words of comfort and peace, and wasn't afraid to talk about the subject everyone else avoided—Lodell's impending death.

Lette was comfortable with the issue of dying. She didn't shy away from talking about its coming, nor did she morbidly dwell on it. She knew that death is best dealt with head-on —fearlessly, confidently, and graciously. She was convinced that for believers, death was simply a transition to a new life—a life lived in the presence of a loving Creator—a life free of pain and sorrow, a life with no cancer, no death, and no good-byes.

Two years prior, on a trip to Houston, incessant, intense coughing had sent seventy-year-old Lodell and her husband to an unfamiliar emergency room. X-rays revealed the unmistakable dark mass in her right lung that was cancer— that creeping foe that would eventually spread to her bones and liver.

Lodell had fought the enemy with everything that was in her. The nurses who administered her chemotherapy had become accustomed to her routine instruction: "Don't you spill one drop. I want it all. I want to live." And they didn't. For they, too, wanted Lodell to live. They were in the fight with her. Everyone who knew her was caught up in her resolve and joined spirits with hers in the battle.

Determined though Lodell had been to beat her adversary, the cancer had overwhelmed her body, and she now was close to death, confined to her bed. The cancer had eaten away her strength, and the powerful morphine that kept her pain to a minimum also kept her in a near-coma condition. The end was near.

Through her daily visits to the Wrights' home, Lette had gained the trust and confidence of the family and friends who helped tend to Lodell's needs. Lette's peace and joy affected everyone in the household.

Nelda, Lodell's sister-in-law and frequent visitor, was familiar with death. She had lost her husband to a heart attack when she was only twenty-nine, and she had spent the last several months caring for a dying aunt. As a nurse of thirty years, she was familiar with death and had herself comforted the dying and their families on many occasions. Yet she was awestruck at the confidence and grace that radiated from Lette and knew that she would carry her impression on her heart the rest of her days.

Lodell's husband, R. L., was a man who took care of things. If there was a problem, he'd fix it. If someone needed help, he was always willing to lend a hand. And his ready smile exuded a cheerful openness that claimed any and all as his friends. Yet for all his confident cheerfulness, he was powerless to "fix" Lodell. He felt useless and hopeless as he witnessed his wife's life ebb away. But seeing the gracious way Lette stood with Lodell in the face of death, he felt a growing sense of peace that lightened his heavy heart.

The couple's children, Tim and Kay, were attentive and caring. When work and family commitments kept them from their mother's side, they were comforted knowing that Lette was there—lovingly serving their mother, tending to every need.

Lette recognized in Lodell the signs of the end: the shallow, irregular breathing; the erratic pulse; the abnormally low blood pressure—Lodell's growing awareness of her impending death.

Lette lightly stroked Lodell's withered hand and spoke words of tenderness and compassion that were for Lodell alone. The family and friends who had gathered to say goodbye had the feeling they were eavesdropping on a deeply private and intimate conversation. And they were.

After speaking her own parting words to her friend, Lette rose to prepare for the coming ceremony—a ceremony she'd arranged for numerous other men and women and boys and girls—a ceremony of parting and hope.

Lette directed the rearranging of the furniture. She placed Lodell's bed in the center and enough chairs around it for each honored participant. Then she motioned for everyone to sit down and sat down herself.

"We're gathered here to honor a beloved friend, wife, mother, and sister-in-law," Lette began. "But more than that, we're here to ease her passing—to guide her over the bridge from this life to the next. Tim," she said, handing Lodell's only son an open Bible, "would you read the Twenty-third Psalm?"

Tim took the Bible from Lette's hand tentatively, swiping at the tear that trickled down his face. His voice wavered as he read:

The LORD is my shepherd; I shall not want. He maketh me to lie down in green pastures: he leadeth me beside the still waters. He restoreth my soul: he leadeth me in the paths of righteousness for his name's sake. Yea, though I walk through the valley of the shadow of death, I will fear no evil: for thou art with me; thy rod and thy staff they comfort me. Thou preparest a table before me in the presence of mine enemies: thou anointest my head with oil; my cup runneth over. Surely goodness and mercy shall follow me all the days of my life: and I will dwell in the house of the LORD for ever.

As he gingerly handed the Bible back to Lette, she turned to address the entire group. "Each of you is here because you've been a blessing to Lodell. Your presence in her life brought her joy, and your love has given her strength. If Lodell could speak to you today, I think I know some of what she'd say."

With that, Lette rose from her chair and faced R. L., placing her hands on his shoulders as she spoke. "R. L., you've been a loyal and faithful companion to Lodell for fifty-three years. Lodell loves you with all her heart and is thankful for the wonderful life she has shared with you. All in this room have witnessed your fierce dedication to watching over and protecting her through this long ordeal. You supervised each treatment, you insisted that she have the best care, and you always, always—" Lette paused, an irrepressible twinkle lighting her eyes, "—you always pressed her caregivers for specific answers to difficult questions. Everyone who took care of Lodell knew you on a first-name basis because you were relentless in ensuring that they paid the utmost attention to her care. You have been her advocate, her protector, and her friend. Today you can bid her farewell, confident that you did everything in your power to help her overcome the sickness that has conquered her body—," she paused again, this time to squeeze R. L.'s shoulders, "—but not her soul."

R. L.'s eyes brimmed with tears as he scooped up Lette and hugged her tight. He had no words, but as he set her down gently, his tearful eyes met hers with an unmistakable look of fondness and gratitude.

Lette approached each remaining loved one in the same confident, gentle manner with which she had addressed R. L. She stood before each person in turn, placing her hands on his or her shoulders, and spoke of Lodell's love and appreciation for their part in her life and her death.

A sense of God's sweet presence filled the air. Each tear-stained face seemed to shine with love and peace in spite of the sad reason for their gathering.

Finally, Lette motioned for everyone to come near Lodell's bed. Following her lead, each participant placed a gentle hand on Lodell's wasted body. Lette bowed her head, and every head in the room bowed reverently with her. Speaking with the confidence of a child who felt at ease in the throne room of her heavenly Father, Lette prayed. She prayed for Lodell's comfort, she prayed for the peace of those surrounding the bed, and she prayed that Lodell would feel released from the confines of her body to fly safely to her Father's arms.

As Lette prayed, Lodell's spirit peacefully left her body as she breathed her last breath. At the conclusion of Lette's prayer, each sorrowful head lifted and looked upward as if to watch Lodell's soul ascending heavenward. Their hearts were heavy with loss, but their spirits were full of hope and assurance.

Those who were honored to share in this solemn ceremony were changed forever. Lette's legacy of peace, comfort, and hope passed sweetly to each soul. And Lette...well, Lette moved on to the next home that needed her tender touch, her vision of eternity, and her legacy of hope.

tenderness

CHAPTER
Five

You are My workmanship, created to do good works, which I've already uniquely prepared in advance for you to accomplish. Whatever you are doing, even if it seems unimportant, work at it with all your heart, like you're passionately doing it for Me. I'll reward you! Commit everything you do to Me. As you trust in Me, watch Me make your life radiantly shine.

Tenderly,

Y O U R
GOD

—from Ephesians 2:10; Colossians 3:23–24; Psalm 37:5–6

Tenderness is seen in the little things you do. In the small kindnesses, in the gentle touches, in the attentive way you listen to problems big and small. It's easy to get caught up in the busyness of your duties and forget to leave behind the fragrance of your tenderness. Yet all you need is a gentle reminder, for tenderness is part of who you are—it's why you chose this profession.

Being tender means being tuned in to others —having your radar turned on so you're ready to sense the needs of those under your care, perhaps even before they voice them. When you're in tune with these needs, you're in a position to *respond.* That's the key to tenderness. And you not only respond to needs, you respond with sensitivity to the unique makeup of each individual.

But always being the tender responder can wear you down and leave you depleted. That's when you need to be replenished by the Great Physician who is always standing by to respond to *your* needs with tenderness and sensitivity. Jesus said sweetly, *"Come to me, all you who are weary and burdened, and I will give you rest. Take my yoke upon you and learn from me, for I am gentle and humble in heart, and you will find rest for your souls"* (Matthew 11:28–29).

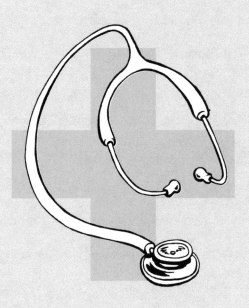

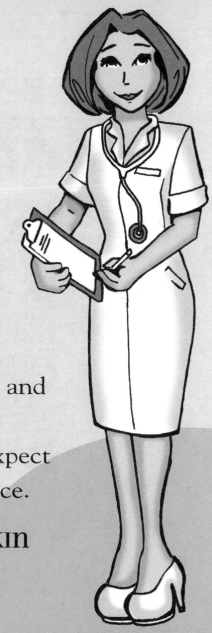

When love and
skill work
together, expect
a masterpiece.

JOHN RUSKIN

Wanda saw this unobtrusive worker tucking in blanket corners and fluffing pillows. She wondered how anyone could be satisfied with such menial tasks.

TECHNICALITIES

Wanda tentatively rounded the corner that led into the cardiac unit of Morehouse General Hospital. She tried to put forth an air of confidence, but the sick feeling in her stomach and the weakness in her knees drained the look of assurance from her eyes. This was her first real shift as a registered nurse. Her three years of training had been difficult, but she had been determined to be among the top 5 percent of her class. And she had done it. Wanda had a knack for memorizing facts and figures, and her head was filled with valuable technical knowledge.

Now, attired in a white cotton smock and pants, she

Tenderness

hesitantly approached the nurses' station. It was 11 P.M. and very quiet. Wanda felt a surprising wave of disappointment wash over her. She'd expected an atmosphere of hustle and bustle—nurses hurrying from room to room, adjusting equipment, handling small emergencies. But the halls were empty, and the only people she saw were two nurses behind the station counter.

"Excuse me," Wanda began, "I'm looking for Ms. Rockwell."

One of the nurses lifted her head and, without a word, nodded toward a woman standing with her back to Wanda. She was bent over a clipboard, busily making notes. Wanda approached nervously.

"Uh, Ms. Rockwell?"

Ms. Rockwell didn't turn from her notes or acknowledge Wanda's presence in any way.

Wanda tried again, speaking louder this time and trying to sound confident. "Ms. Rockwell!"

Wanda's first-day jitters made her overcorrect the volume of her voice, and Ms. Rockwell's head jerked up with a start as her clipboard clattered to the floor. Wanda now had her supervisor's full attention, but the angry look in her eyes made Wanda want to melt into the wall.

After retrieving her clipboard, Ms. Rockwell turned and faced Wanda squarely. "What are you yelling about, young lady!" Ms. Rockwell barked. "Don't you know we have a wing full of very sick patients? Keep your voice down!" she shouted, noticeably exceeding the volume for which she chastised her new charge. "Who are you, anyway?"

Every ounce of composure Wanda had managed to muster was shattered. She was near tears but quickly resolved not to give in to them. "I'm Wanda—Wanda Johnson. I'm the new nurse. Mr. Walters told me to report to you."

"Oh, great," Ms. Rockwell grumbled as she rolled her eyes in exaggerated exasperation. "Another rookie. Why does that man continue to put inexperienced nurses on *my* shift? I don't have time to play wet nurse to every new nurse he graduates," she proclaimed to no one in particular.

Then she placed both hands on her hips. "All right, if I must deal with you…Marge! Come over here and show Ms.…what did you say your name was?"

Tenderness

"Wanda Johnson."

"Marge, take Ms. Johnson with you on your rounds tonight. Don't let her get too close to anything, but let her watch you as you work. And Ms. Johnson," she said, turning to Wanda, "try not to upset any of the patients or our work routines. Just stay out of the way and watch!"

"Yes ma'am," Wanda answered feebly. She wished Ms. Rockwell knew how dedicated she was to learning all the technical aspects of nursing. She had excelled in school, easily learning and applying information about disease processes, the newest medicines, and the latest treatments. She had been thrilled to be placed in the state's most technologically advanced hospital, one that used the most up-to-date equipment and procedures. This hadn't been the beginning she had imagined.

In spite of her humiliating "welcome," Wanda was soon caught up in the excitement of the many humming and beeping machines connected to ailing patients throughout the unit. She studied the labels on the IV pouches and watched the monitors to learn all she could about the status of various patients. She would show Ms. Rockwell! She would soon know all there was to know about the procedures and equipment of this unit. She had an analytical mind and assimilated information quickly.

Marge, her guide for the evening, was the epitome of efficiency—something Wanda admired immensely. She moved briskly from post to post, checking vitals, taking readings from monitors, changing out empty bags of medicinal fluids, and resetting beeping machines. If a patient had a request, she filled it quickly and professionally. She answered questions matter-of-factly and made sure all scheduled medicines and treatments were administered properly and on time.

As Wanda and Marge moved from room to room, Wanda kept noticing a mousy little woman whom she presumed to be a nurse's aide. Throughout her rounds, Wanda saw this unobtrusive worker emptying bedpans, tucking in stray blanket corners, and fluffing flattened pillows. Wanda wondered how anyone could be satisfied with such menial tasks when surrounded by advanced technology and equipment. *Oh, well,* she thought. *I guess someone has to do the menial work.*

Tenderness

About 2 A.M. Marge took a short break, leaving Wanda on her own for a few minutes. Remembering Ms. Rockwell's warning not to upset anything, Wanda strolled through the halls, dreaming of the day when she would be entrusted with the tools of medical science. As she walked and dreamed, she slowly became aware of the sound of voices coming from a room a couple of doors down. She approached and paused in the doorway, peering into the darkness and listening to the quiet conversation.

"Fran, could you smooth out the sheet under my back?"

"Of course, Mrs. Heath, I'd be glad to."

"Who would think such an insignificant wrinkle could make a person so miserable? It's just that these bedsores on my scrawny back are so easily irritated."

As Wanda's eyes adjusted to the dim light, she watched the nurse's aide she'd seen earlier as she gently rolled the patient to her side and smoothed the badly wadded sheet. No wonder Mrs. Heath was so uncomfortable. The sheet had gotten all twisted and lumpy and would have made any-one uncomfortable, much less this fragile, elderly woman.

"Let me put some salve on those sores," the wispy-haired young woman offered as she pushed her glasses back up on her nose. "It'll make you feel better."

"I don't know how I would have survived these last few nights without you, Fran," the woman said with grateful affection. "You always seem to know just what I need. And I know I'm not the only one you help. I listen to you tending to the needs of the patients on either side of me and across the hall, and I know how much your tender touch means to all of us. You have a real gift. You sense the needs that are deeper than our physical ailments. You comfort our spirits, Fran. You calm our fears and bring peace to our souls."

As Wanda soaked in this touching scene, the eyes of her heart were opened to new truths—she glimpsed a world of knowledge beyond the tangible and technical.

As she finished her first shift, puttering alongside capable Marge, she began to actually *look* at the people in the beds. She watched their faces and saw them wince with discomfort in their sleep. She made eye contact with those who were awake and tried to communicate warmth and concern with her eyes. In response to her tender outreach, she saw appreciation reflected in weary eyes. She saw weak smiles of gratitude and heard muted sighs of relief. She saw an obvious appreciation that someone had noticed—that someone cared.

And she was amazed at how much could be learned from someone trained only in the techniques of tenderness.

empathy

CHAPTER
SIX

Look to Me and My strength, always seeking
Me. I'm your hiding place. I'll protect you
from trouble and surround you with
songs of deliverance. When you put
your hope in Me, I'll renew your
strength. I'll help you to soar above
your circumstances. I comfort you in
every situation so that you can comfort
those in any trouble with the comfort
you have received from Me.

Understanding hugs,
YOUR GOD OF
aLL HOPe

—from Psalms 105:4; 32:7; Isaiah 40:31; 2 Corinthians 1:3–9

Empathy is a precious trait, but it comes at a price—a high price. Sympathy is a sweet expression of caring and concern about another's pain. But empathy is truly understanding that pain because you've been there yourself. And it's empathy that we all yearn for when we're in deep pain.

Each of us has experienced pain in some form. And pain of all kinds shares some common characteristics. Understanding these characteristics is part of what makes *you* an empathetic caregiver.

First, pain hurts. As simple as that sounds, it's true. Whether the pain is physical, emotional, mental, or spiritual—it hurts. Second, severe pain incapacitates. It puts your patients in bed, and that can be frustrating. Third, it demands attention. It screams to be made better—now! Fourth, pain wears people down; it absolutely exhausts us in every way. And finally, pain seeks relief. That's why hurting people are under your care.

No life is free of pain—not even yours. But the pain you've experienced, as unpleasant as it may have been, has produced in you the beautiful fruit of empathy. Nursing is a profession in which even the most painful experiences of life can be used to bring health and healing to others through your gift of empathy.

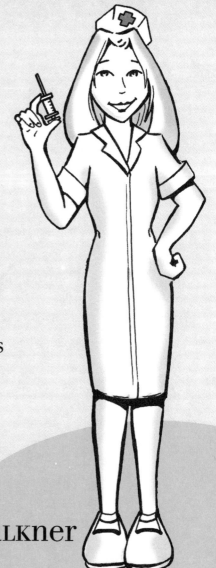

Somehow
tragedy reveals
itself to fellow
sufferers—the
empathy leaps
the gap.

DR. PAUL FAULKNER

Marilyn knew how it
worked. What she hadn't
known was how it felt.
Now she knew.

Bad Hair Day

Marilyn stood in the shower, her tears mingling with the water that ran down her face. She stared at the clump of brown hair that lay wet and limp in her hand. It was happening. Even though she had seen it happen to countless patients under her care, even though she had known it was likely to happen to her, the sight of her own hair in her hand filled her with a desperate sort of panic she hadn't expected.

Marilyn was an oncology nurse at St. Francis Hospital. She'd worked with cancer patients for ten years. She'd seen patients of all ages and stations in life go through the ordeal of cancer. She'd learned that the disease was no respecter of persons. It could hit anyone—at any time. Some people got well. Some didn't. She'd seen it all. She knew how it worked.

What she hadn't known was how it felt.

Now she knew.

It felt helpless. It felt out of control. It felt overpowering and frightening.

This new insight had made her a better nurse already. Until now she had always felt like someone on the outside looking in. She'd felt sympathy for her patients—sorry that anyone had to go through such a trial. But now she could actually feel her patients' pain. Her sympathy had become empathy.

She put her head back under the water and used her other hand to help rinse away the shampoo. Another clump of dark locks clung to her fingers.

She'd always gotten compliments on her beautiful hair. "You've got 'good hair,'" the hairstylists said. Her hair was thick and wavy and vibrant. At least it used to be. Her hair was like her mother's, and she loved being like her mother.

Even at seventy-six, her mother's hair was still thick and black, with only a few scattered gray hairs that served as witnesses to the authentic color of their companions.

With the second handful of hair, silent tears flooded her cheeks. The sob that welled up in her chest caught in her throat. Her heart instinctively cried heavenward. *God,* she prayed, *I know You're out there somewhere, but I need to know that You're here—with me. I need to sense Your presence. I feel so alone. Please reveal Your love to me.*

How many times had she tried to comfort patients of faith to rely on God in their times of pain? How many times had she said, almost flippantly, "God is with you. He cares about your pain. If you'll just ask Him to reveal His presence to you, He surely will." Those words echoed hollowly in her mind now, sounding empty and cold.

Stifling her tears, Marilyn tried to regain her composure. Oddly, her mind went instantly to her favorite hymn—"It Is Well with My Soul." The song had been her brother's favorite. When he died of a sudden heart attack at the age of forty-one, she'd adopted it as her own. She hummed its tune as she finished her shower.

empathy

Marilyn put on some comfortable Capri slacks and her favorite comfy T-shirt and walked slowly, sadly into the garage to find her husband. She and Paul had celebrated their thirtieth anniversary last August. He was her best friend and the first one she went to when she had news to share—good or bad.

Paul was bent over a lathe, as he often was on a Saturday afternoon, turning a piece of oak for one of the legs of the bed he was crafting for Marilyn's birthday next month. Paul had inherited his touch for woodworking from a grandfather who died before he was born. Marilyn loved to see him at work. He always looked strong and peaceful when he had a piece of wood in his hands—attributes she was most lacking at the moment.

"Paul," she called above the buzz of the lathe. Paul flipped off the machine and turned to meet her with an easy smile. She couldn't help but return a smile of her own, weak though it was. He quickly read the pain in her eyes, and in two long strides he had her in his arms.

"What's wrong, sweetie?" he asked gently.

In reply, she held out her clenched fist, palm up, and opened it slowly to reveal her shiny, wet hair.

"Oh, honey, I'm so sorry."

Marilyn sobbed softly in the comfort of his strong arms. "I've seen so many other people go through this. I've been the one at the other end of the line, administering this awful chemo to *other* people. But now it's me. Now I have this 'poison' flowing through *my* body, wreaking havoc with my immune system, and killing off *all my hair!* Just a few minutes ago, in the shower, I felt more alone than I think I ever have before. Seeing clumps of hair in my hands was solid evidence that this cancer is having its way with me. That it is out of my control. I felt so alone…" Her voice trailed off as she realized that her last statement might make Paul feel that he wasn't being there for her, that he wasn't doing all he should to make her feel protected and loved. One look into his deep, brown eyes told her she was right.

"Oh, Paul…" She was sobbing again. "I don't mean I felt alone because you aren't there. I know *you're* here for me. I always know that. It's just that…" Marilyn struggled to put

empathy

words to the pain in her heart. "It's just that I don't feel that *God* is with me. I know I shouldn't even say those words, but that's how I feel. Can you understand any of this?" Marilyn asked, locking eyes with her handsome husband.

Paul returned her gaze, then pulled her tight into his arms. "I don't understand exactly what you feel—I can't. I've never been through what you're going through. But I do know that I love you with or without hair. You are as beautiful to me today as you were the day I married you. I love *you*—and *you* are a lot more than a head of hair. Besides," he said, pulling back from her so his twinkling eyes could look into hers, "I've seen pictures of you when you were a baby, and your head was as bald and shiny as a brass doorknob. God covered your head with hair then, and He'll do it again once we get through this chemo."

Marilyn didn't know how he did it, but some of Paul's strength always transferred to her when he held her in his arms. Still, as she walked back into the kitchen, she felt the stab of isolation once more. She knew Paul was with her, but she couldn't feel God. Where was He? Why did He feel so far away?

BAD HAIR DAY

She reached up to run her fingers through her hair and felt raw emotion rise in her chest again, bringing fresh tears to her eyes. Her breath caught in her throat, and she felt as though she couldn't breathe. Bracing herself on the edge of the kitchen sink, she looked out the window toward the sky. Her heart cried out, *Where are You, God? Do You hear me? Do You see my pain? Do You even care?*

Filled with anguish, she closed her eyes and dropped her head. How could she go to work and face her now "fellow" cancer patients? What hope, what compassion, what peace could she extend to them when she had none of her own?

Finally opening her eyes, she determined to get on with her day—whether God was with her or not. She had a few hours before her shift started at three, and she didn't want to waste her whole day crying. She walked dejectedly to the counter that held her daily calendar to see what needed to be taken care of before she went to work.

Her eyes fell almost immediately to the daily scripture at the bottom of the page: *Don't be concerned about the outward beauty that depends on fancy hairstyles, expensive jewelry, or beautiful clothes. You should be known for the beauty that comes*

BAD HAIR DAY

She reached up to run her fingers through her hair and felt raw emotion rise in her chest again, bringing fresh tears to her eyes. Her breath caught in her throat, and she felt as though she couldn't breathe. Bracing herself on the edge of the kitchen sink, she looked out the window toward the sky. Her heart cried out, *Where are You, God? Do You hear me? Do You see my pain? Do You even care?*

Filled with anguish, she closed her eyes and dropped her head. How could she go to work and face her now "fellow" cancer patients? What hope, what compassion, what peace could she extend to them when she had none of her own?

Finally opening her eyes, she determined to get on with her day—whether God was with her or not. She had a few hours before her shift started at three, and she didn't want to waste her whole day crying. She walked dejectedly to the counter that held her daily calendar to see what needed to be taken care of before she went to work.

Her eyes fell almost immediately to the daily scripture at the bottom of the page: *Don't be concerned about the outward beauty that depends on fancy hairstyles, expensive jewelry, or beautiful clothes. You should be known for the beauty that comes*

99

from within, the unfading beauty of a gentle and quiet spirit, which is so precious to God" (1 Peter 3:3–4).

The words seemed to jump off the page and into her heart: "Don't be concerned about the outward beauty that depends on fancy hairstyles!" She knew without a doubt that those words were explicitly for her at that exact moment.

For the fourth time that day, she wept. But this time it was different. This time, she definitely felt the presence of God. And she knew that she was precious to Him. This simple message, these simple words were for her, from Him.

A delightful awareness began to dawn in Marilyn's heart: From her experiences as a patient, she was learning rich lessons of great value—lessons that would make her a better caregiver, a better nurse.

Marilyn squared her shoulders and lifted her head, a smile forming on her lips. She felt a new determination to extend compassion, hope, and an awareness of God's presence to the patients she would greet in just a few hours.

She was going to make it after all.

tlc

CHAPTER
seven

101

I've chosen you. You are deeply loved and cherished. I've equipped you to humbly and patiently practice tender-hearted mercy and kindness to others. Don't lose heart or grow weary in demon-strating tender loving care. You'll make a difference if you don't give up.

Patiently,

YOUR FATHER OF

aBUNDaNT LIFe

—from Colossians 3:12; Galatians 6:9

It has often been said that the most important medicine a nurse can give is TLC—tender loving care. This doesn't detract from the significance of the amazing treatments and technological advances with which we're blessed in this age.

But none of that can replace your loving care. Often you are the one who listens, who touches, who takes time to explain. Because you possess that wonderful blend of technical knowledge and personal care, you earn the *trust* of those for whom you care. Not only do you deal with the patients under your care, but you also deal with their worried—and sometimes demanding—

family members. You become the link between technology and real life. You are the caregiver.

The very word *caregiver* says much about who you are. Truly caring about another human being requires an investment of self—emotionally, physically, and mentally. And that's what you do every day: You invest yourself in others because you *care* about them. You care about their pain, their comfort, their health. And because you care, you *give* of yourself—over and over, all day long, day in and day out.

You are the embodiment of TLC. Hugs to you!

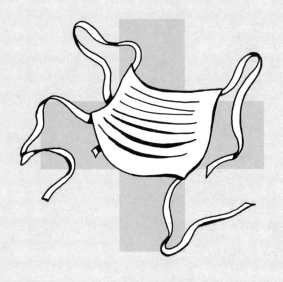

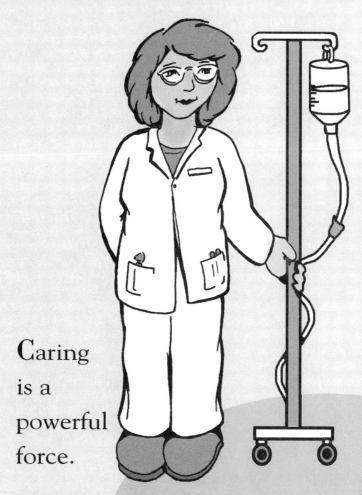

Caring
is a
powerful
force.

FRANK REED

Something told Nellie
that this was more than
ordinary homesickness.

nellie's cure

Beads of salty sweat dripped from Nellie's face as she bent down to look the sobbing eight-year-old in the eye. "I don't feel good! My tummy aches!" little, red-faced Jason howled. "I want to go home! I want my mommy!" With each proclamation, Jason's wailing escalated in pitch and intensity.

Jason's bewildered counselor stood by helplessly as Nurse Nellie spoke soothingly to the sobbing, nearly hysterical little boy.

It usually happened just about this time. After the day's activities had ended and the evening devotions and prayers were concluded, weary counselors would tuck excited, wide-awake campers into bed, trying to settle them down to sleep.

TLC

Then, after most of the exhausted troupers finally succumbed to much-needed sleep, the attacks of homesickness would begin. There were at least one or two severe cases every session. But something told Nellie that this was more than ordinary homesickness.

"It's OK, Jason. Come on inside the nurse's hut with me," she soothed him. "I'm sure we can make you feel better. Go on back to your cabin, Ronnie," she told the grateful seventeen-year-old counselor. "I'll bring Jason back when he feels better."

"I don't want to go back!" Jason moaned, "I want to go hooomme!"

"Never mind," Nellie cooed as she led Jason up the steps. "We'll get it figured out."

Once inside the nurse's hut, Nellie put on her most professional manner. She had found that children—and even adults—could be somewhat in awe of nurses and that the best way to help an ailing heart was to start with a surface physical exam. Once that was done, she could usually offer what she considered the most important therapy of all: tender loving care.

"Come over here, Jason, and sit on my stool," she instructed.

Still sobbing, but with less hysteria, Jason obeyed.

"Stick out your tongue and say 'Ahhh.'"

Jason obliged, though pitiful tears still ran down his cheeks.

"Now turn your head this way so I can look in your ears."

Jason turned, first to the left, then to the right, as Nellie examined his ears.

"Well, I'm relieved to report that your ears and your throat look good. No problems there. But let's listen to your heart. You know, the heart is one of the most important organs in your body."

Jason nodded knowingly, tears beginning to dry up.

"Now, the stethoscope will be a little cold, but I can tell by how you're getting control of yourself that you're a very brave boy and won't mind at all."

Again, Jason nodded his head.

Nellie placed the stethoscope on his bare chest and listened intently for a few seconds. "My!" she exclaimed. "You have a wonderfully strong heartbeat! But I should have known you would, just to look at you. Jason, you seem to be a very strong and healthy boy! But I do seem to remember that you said you had a tummy ache. Does your tummy still ache a little?"

TLC

Jason nodded.

"Well, I have some of the best medicine there is for tummy aches!" Turning to her medicine cabinet, Nellie opened both doors wide to reveal an impressive array of "nurse stuff." "Here it is!" she said with a flourish, "Pepto-Bismol! The best there is! All it takes is one big spoonful and a few minutes of rest on my special nurse's bed, and your tummy will be as good as new."

Jason almost smiled.

Once Nellie had Jason comfortably situated in the soft bed with the soft comforter, she pulled a chair up beside him and began to administer her special treatment of TLC.

"Jason, when we were talking outside the cabin earlier, you said you wanted to go home. I'll bet you really love your family. Why don't you tell me a little about them while we wait for the Pepto-Bismol to make your tummy feel better."

"Well, I have a sister—she's littler than me. Her name is Sarah. She's the reason I want to go home. I need to take care of her."

"Now, Jason, I'm sure your mommy and daddy do a perfectly good job of taking care of your little sister."

At this, Jason's face clouded and tears began falling again in earnest.

"What is it, Jason? What's wrong?" Nellie pleaded.

"My—my—daddy—" Jason couldn't get the words out.

"It's OK, Jason, take your time," Nellie reassured him.

"My daddy died!" the words finally tumbled out.

"Oh, Jason," Nellie said, reaching down and hugging her little patient. "I'm so sorry. I'm so very sorry. I know you must miss him very much, and I'll bet you're a wonderful big brother to Sarah."

"I try to be," Jason sobbed, "but she cries 'cause she misses him, and I don't know how to make her feel better. And my mom—she cries too. I hear her crying every night—she cries loud. I never knew grownups cried like that. So I try to be brave and not let her see me cry. Somebody's got to be brave. Daddy would want me to be strong. When he used to go on trips, he always told me to take care of my little sister and my mommy—'You're the man of the family,' he'd say. But I don't feel like a man. I miss him too. I miss him so bad…" Jason's voice trailed off, and he began sobbing anew.

TLC

Nellie pulled him onto her lap and rocked him back and forth like a baby until his crying subsided. Then she took his shoulders and held him at arm's length so she could look him squarely in the eyes.

"Jason, you really *are* a very brave boy," Nellie told Jason kindly. "But being brave doesn't mean that you can't tell your mommy you're sad or that you can't let her see you cry. Your mommy loves you very much, and she knows that you're sad. She won't think you're not brave if you cry. She'll understand; I promise she will.

"But I want to tell you something even more important, Jason, and this is something you need to keep in your heart for the rest of your life. There are two parts to what I'm going to tell you, and both of these parts are true. First of all, your daddy will always be your daddy. Even though he's not here on earth, he'll always be in your heart, and he'll always be in your mind. He will always be your daddy.

"The next thing is this: God is your Father too. Really, He's everyone's Father, but the Bible says that He's a special kind of Father to boys and girls who don't have daddies here on earth. A long time ago, He sent us a message in the Bible that says He is 'a father to the fatherless.' In one way,

Jason, you are fatherless. And so in a very special way, *God* is your Daddy. In a way more special than He is Daddy to all the other boys and girls who have their daddies still with them.

"Knowing this won't take away the hurt—it won't keep you from missing your daddy, but it will help fill the hole in your heart."

Jason's crying was limited now to a few intermittent sobs. His round, innocent eyes looked into Nellie's face for answers, desperate for the truth. "But Nurse Nellie, how do you *know* that God can help fill this hole in my heart? How do you *know* He can be a special Daddy to me?"

"I know because my own daddy died when I was a little girl. I was just about Sarah's age. I didn't have a big brother like you to help take care of me, but I had a mommy who cried, and I cried too. It was my Sunday school teacher who told me about God being my special Daddy—about His being a father to the fatherless. I have to tell you the truth, Jason. I *still* miss my daddy, even though I'm a grownup. The hole in my heart never closed up all the way, but having God as my special Daddy always makes me feel a little safer, a little more special, and a whole lot more loved."

TLC

Nellie tapped Jason's chest gently with her finger. "Keep these words in your heart and say them to yourself every day: 'My God is a Father to the fatherless. I have *two* daddies who love me.'"

Jason wrapped both arms around Nellie's neck and hugged her tightly. "My tummy feels much better now. I think I can go back to my cabin. I'm never, *ever* going to forget your special words—and I'm going to teach them to my little sister too. Thanks, Nurse Nellie."

Serve wholeheartedly,
as if you were
serving the Lord,…
because you know
that the Lord will reward
everyone for whatever
good he does.

EPHESIANS 6:7

Look for these other *Hugs* books: